THE SEVEN POM

C000120046

Colin Teevan

THE SEVEN POMEGRANATE SEEDS

OBERON BOOKS
LONDON

WWW.OBERONBOOKS.COM

First published in 2014 by Oberon Books Ltd
521 Caledonian Road, London N7 9RH
Tel: +44 (0) 20 7607 3637 / Fax: +44 (0) 20 7607 3629
e-mail: info@oberonbooks.com
www.oberonbooks.com

A catalogue record for this book is available from the British Library.

PB ISBN: 978-1-78319-131-4
E ISBN: 978-1-78319-630-2

Cover image: Hades abducting Persephone, from a wall painting in the small royal tomb at Verghina (Vergina), Macedonia, 4th century B.C.

For my mother, Pauline.

Introduction

If not in the front rank in terms of quality this will at least be one of the cheekiest inaugural lectures, in that I, the laureate designate, will in large part not be giving it.

This comes not from the desire to shirk my responsibilities, welcome by-product though that is, but from the pathology of a playwright or screenwriter.

I write words for other people to say.

In fact I write words for other people pretending to be other people I have imagined to say to other people I have imagined, witnessed by yet other people, this time ones I hope I don't have to imagine, sitting watching them in the dark or behind a recording device, or in front of a screen. I have been doing this for twenty-five years, and it has become the way I think about things. I do not write drama to send messages. Why would a playwright know more about anything than anyone else? I write drama to discover what I think about the difficult things, the contradictory things, the intractable things; war, love, desire, death and how these things manifest themselves in the world around us.

And when one has had the good fortune, as I have had, to have so many great actors, such as those you will see tonight, perform one's words, with such accuracy, craft, generosity of spirit and presence, one becomes only too aware of one's own shortcomings as a performer of one's own words.

However, out of solidarity with these brilliant performers, and so that this is not the actual cheekiest lecture – that is the one where I do not appear at all, the death of the lecturer one might call it, the author's revenge on Roland Barthes – I will say a few words about the origins of *The Seven Pomegranate Seeds*.

The play, or monologue cycle, is the result of a long conversation between Euripides and me. It was through Euripides I came to drama. Literature always encourages one to read drama as literature, thematically, socio-historically, politically. Playwrights however write for the stage. This might seem obvious but it is something often forgotten by the literary critic. Playwrights write for the performer existing in three-dimensional space, in actual time, witnessed by an audience. The text must contain the information required to animate not only the characters' speech, but also the playing space, and negotiate the relationship between the imaginary space and the audience.

And it was translating the *Iphigenia in Aulis* line by line, aged 16, under the beady eye of an octogenarian Jesuit, that I learnt how the dramatic line, the action contained within the line, the scene, the characters' characteristics and trajectory, and the plot structure were encrypted into the play text.

So Euripedes and I go back a long way.

But this particular piece grew out of a 2005 series of monologues for men I had written. *Missing Persons; Roy Keane and Other Tragedies* which was performed in the West End by Greg Hicks, was loosely based on Greek sources. It contained one monologue directly drawn from Euripides, 'The Last Word'. This was a contemporary inversion of the Medea myth in which a man murders his children to be revenged on his wife. This was the piece that most satisfied me and seemed to signal a direction of travel. So later that year when Professor Oliver Taplin and Helen Eastman asked me to write a piece for the inauguration of the Onassis Programme at Oxford, I suggested a cycle of monologues for women, a companion piece for *Missing Persons*, this time all based on Euripidean sources dealing with mothers and children[1].

Euripides, for someone who allegedly hated women, created some of the most memorable female roles in the dramatic canon[2]. It's true, he didn't create them for women, since women weren't allowed to perform in the public theatre and some believe they weren't even allowed to attend dramatic performances and, if they were, it seems unlikely they would have sat with the men. It's also true that a memorable role doesn't equate to a happy ending and most of his female characters have memorable but not particularly happy endings. Especially the mothers – apart from those represented tonight, there is a whole Trojan cycle of plays, nearly all of which explore the tragedy of war, exile, death through the woman's and most especially, the mother's perspective. It has been suggested that Euripides' depiction of women, to be performed by men, possibly only in front of men, expressed the anxiety of Athenian male society of the feminine they generally excluded from public spaces and office. Or perhaps it is a fear of what women, and especially mothers, understood. They did something men could not do, they had babies. And as a result of losing

---

1. While Persephone and Demeter do not appear as characters in the extant plays, their presence in both choruses and as mythical exemplars is evident in many plays, not least *Electra, Helen* and *Ion*.
2. In popular accounts, Euripedes met his end by being dismembered by a horde of women irate at his portrayal of them. This demise however in imitation of that of Pentheus in his final play, *The Bacchae*, is highly unlikely since *The Bacchae* was first staged posthumously.

these babies, they understood a second thing that men could not – what it is to lose a child you have borne. And in that they understood the true cost of war, of death, of exile. A thing to be feared indeed, they understood the true cost of the world man, by and large, had created. They are the ones who invariably are left to pick up the pieces; The Women of Troy, Hecuba, Andromache. Even when it is the mother who commits the outrage as in *Hypsipyle, Ion, Bacchae* or even arguably *Medea*, the outrage is committed in response to a male outrage, and the mother more often than not is the one left to live with the consequences.

But it wasn't this that drew me to these stories of Euripides. Something else about his work resonated for me in a very contemporary way; the sheer amount of missing or dead children. His extant oeuvre reads almost as one single piece of perpetual loss. And we seemed in 2006, and continue to seem now, to be a society living in an age of anxiety about children. Back then there had yet to be the McCann case, the Fritzl case, the Castro case; and Natascha Kampusch was only discovered the summer after this play's first performance. Yet it shocks me, returning to them this year, how much these stories seem to foreshadow these cases. This is not to say I knew anything more than anyone else about these things then or now. If I did I would articulate it for you in a proper paper or lecture. But I did not know what to think. However, from the Moor's murders and the Bulger case, to the Louise Woodward case and the constant revelations of child abuse that were then emerging almost weekly in my native Ireland that formed the sociological back drop to these stories; to the stories the first performer of this, Clare Higgins told me of her life; and my also being then a young father, or at least a younger father than I am today, I knew that this discourse about children was important, that it said something about us and the world we lived in.

And to think about it I had this conversation with Euripides.

And I wrote some words for people I imagined to say, sometimes to other imaginary people, or imaginary gods, sometimes simply to be witnessed by you, sitting out there, in the dark.

Colin Teevan, May 2014

The Seven Pomegranate Seeds was originally commissioned by the Onassis Programme for the Performance of Greek Drama at Oxford University. It was first performed on 21 May 2006 at The Oxford Playhouse by the following company:

PERSEPHONE/HYPSIPYLE/MEDEA/ALCESTIS/PHEDRA/
CREUSA/DEMETER
Clare Higgins

Director Colin Teevan
Producer/Designer Helen Eastman
Production Co-Ordinator Eleanor Lloyd
Dramaturg Jack Bradley
Lighting Designer Neill Brinkworth

The Seven Pomegranate Seeds was revived in this form as the author's professorial inaugural on 11 June 2014 at Birkbeck, University of London by the following company:

PERSEPHONE, Hannah Silva – dir. Nicholas Pitt
HYPSIPYLE, Daisy Lewis – dir. Tom Birch
MEDEA, Rebecca Lenkiewicz – dir. Tyrrell Jones
ALCESTIS, Ann O'Neill – dir. Stephen Darcy
PHEDRA, Jemma Redgrave – dir. Sadie Spencer
CREUSA, Gabrielle Reidy – dir. Charlotte Lewis
DEMETER, Jemma Redgrave – dir. George Want

Curatorial Director Harry Williams
Producer Sophie Larsmon
Projection Designer Duncan McLean
Sound Designer Jo Walker

1. Persephone

under the ground

Summer,
And the Girl –
Not me, you must understand, another girl,
Another time, another world,
Where it was always summer –
And the Girl had no need of sanctuary:
A place of safety, bounded by stones,
Set apart from the world of men.
The world was haven to her.
Barefoot across the moors,
Through the tall grass, and corn, and wild flowers
She ran free.

The birds were her friends,
She gave them names: Sea Spray, Sweet River, Hidden One.
And lineages: 'You are the daughters of the dark ocean
That flows between this world and the next.'
And like a bird the Girl darts this way and that –
I see her now –
As if following the threads of glinting webs
Woven between the heads of golden corn
That lead to the spider's secret store.
The Girl follows the threads around her head,
Her own secret store of stories.
And if a story takes a turning for the worse,
Or a character she herself has conjured up, shocks her

With a sudden, incomprehensible capacity for cruelty,
Or worse, she shocks herself
With the feelings that she harbours in her skinny breast,
She shouts: 'Pax!'
And like a starling changes tack
Seeking out another story thread,
That wipes all memory of previous thoughts dead.

Her mother said:
'Your imagination will be the death of you,
You must watch out,
There are more things in this world than birds to worry about.'
'But I danced this world into being,' said the Girl,
'And now this world dances just for me.'
She gave her mother a quick peck upon the cheek,
'Why should I fear for anything? I have you
And the bread you put upon my plate.'

And with that the Girl was up and off,
Across the garden, out the gate
And up to the moors once more.

'Your shoes, child, you forgot your shoes!
And don't forget what I have said to you!
Please don't lose…
Your way.'

The afternoon burned red and gold,
The ochre earth was cooked and cracked with heat,

Even the corn was weary
With the day-long effort of straining towards the sun.
Upon a mound the Girl sat down
And rubbed her blistered feet.
Her friends, the birds, still flashed around her:
Sea Spray, Sweet River, Hidden One.
Tireder now,
She watched them as they chased
Flies from flower to flower
For one last feed before they sleep.
That's when the thought occurred to her
She should pick some for her mother:
Dog-rose, thyme, lavender.
She made a basket of her dress:
Poppy and –
How strange to see this time of year?
She had to shade her eyes from the lowering sun –
But it was, yes!
Narcissi, a hundred heads sprouting from a single root.
Their sweet smell hung in the evening air and
For what seemed like a whole setting of the sun, she stared at them.
Then, slowly, the Girl –
This other girl
Not me, you must remember –
Slowly, trembling, she stooped
And reached to pick…

Later she would blame herself;
If she hadn't looked at it so long,
If she hadn't stood there making a basket of her dress,
Revealing all,

If she hadn't wanted more than anything
These strange, unseasonal flowers –

But, as her hand touched a stem,
The stems and heads seemed to become
So many fingers of some giant hand
Coming from beneath the ground,
Closing in a massive fist around her fingers.
It gripped her small white hand tight,
And, though she pulled with all her might,
And shouted: 'Leave me,
Leave me alone whoever you are!'
The earth beneath her feet seemed to drain away,
And cracked then cleaved then yawned open wide.
And though she shouted: 'Pax! Pax! Pax!'
The story still took a turning for the worse.
With a rush of air
That sounded like a hundred ghostly horses breaking loose,
She fell down,
Down,
Down into the heart of a burial mound,
And the long dead ancient world below.

—<o>—

Night time, it's late,
And the Mother stands by the garden gate.
She thinks she hears a distant cry
Of her child in pain,
But then all is quiet once again,
And she waits, and waits.
Finally, when she cannot bear it any more,

She goes from neighbour's door to neighbour's door.

'Have you seen her? Have you seen my child?'

She tries not to let her mounting panic show,
But her face is twisted with fear
That bubbles up from below.
Her neighbours shrink from her:
'No I haven't seen her, no.'

She ran out beyond the town
Into the countryside beyond,
To where the birds flew this way and that,
Through the night-time sky.
The air seemed full of rumour.
'Who's taken her?' she cried,
'What Harpie has snatched her away from me?
I always feared her dreaming would lead to this.'
'Perhaps it's not as bad as you imagine,'
She could hear them say, 'Perhaps she's lost
Or has just run away?'
'My child would not run away from me,'
The Mother cried as she ran across the moors
And as she ran she felt herself somehow become a bird
That rose up above the land.
She'd search every centimetre on the surface of the earth.

—◦—

When at length the Girl had finished coughing

And the last of the dust was settling,
She looked around.
At first…
Nothing.

She squinted in the gloom and groped –
Something hard, and flat, and then a corner.
It appeared to be some kind of room.
A room, under the ground?

'What was that?'

She turned.
A sound.

'Who's there?
There's someone there,
I can hear you breathing.
Where is this you've taken me?
My mother warned me about people such as you.
My mother told me what to do.'

Crack,
Something snapped beneath her foot;
A twig.
She reached down,
Her hand caressed the smoothness of a human bone.

'Where is this?
Where is this I am?'

Wildly she looked around and
In the darkness, she began to see...
Shapes.

'Who are you? Get away from me!'

But they do not reply.
She stretches out her hand to try and touch them
Whoever they might be –
Lines
Etched upon the walls,
She traces one with her finger
And is surprised to find it forms
A figure.
A woman sitting on a rock.
Head lowered. She knows this story:
A woman grieving for her child.
Three more women stand behind,
Faces who cannot bear to look.
Then, on to another wall.
Here she traces a galloping horse that
Pulls a chariot and following
The thread of an ancient line, she finds
The lost child,
Her arms waving wildly in the air
As hers must have when she'd fallen down here.

But this girl is half-dressed,
Her purple robe wrenched down about her waist,
Her face twisted,
Her arms stretching for help that doesn't come,
Or something that she cannot bear to leave behind,
And around her small breast is another hand –

'What's that?'

There it was again, the sound.

'Who's there?'

Whoever it is does not respond.
She follows the line from the hand
Around the Girl's back
To the broad shoulders,
A mane of hair and beard blowing in the wind
And down the right arm to the hand
Which holds the whip and reins with which
He drives the chariot at its furious pace.
But his face, what about his face?
She tries to touch them but…
His eyes are empty.

'I know there's someone there.
Where's this you've taken me?'

But no longer is her voice full of defiance.
The violence of this other girl being snatched away

The tiredness, the hunger, the fall, the dust, the shock –
She sits down upon an upturned pot and sobs.

And it seemed the women on the walls sobbed with her too,
Until a voice, close and warm, rasped in her ear:

'Shut up with your tears'

'I'll stop, I'll stop, just tell me who you are and – '

'Shut up,' said the voice, 'not a word
Or I'll have to hurt you.'

'But please,' said the Girl, 'all I want to do is go home?
Let me out, please let me out!'

A rough hand closed across her mouth.

◄o►

The Mother sat down too.
On a rock, on the outskirts of town,
The Girl's shoes set before her.
Nine times she'd flown around the world
But not a trace of her she'd found,

Nor heard a word,
So she had returned.
She now looked like an old woman.
Her neighbours no longer knew her.
'Come in, come in from out there,
You'll catch your death
The summer will soon be at an end.'

But she said:
'Give me one of your babies to hold,
While you see to the harvest.'

They looked from her old cracked hands
To their babies and,
Mumbling excuses, moved away.

It was after that there came the sudden, shocking
Cold.
The land froze, the corn turned black.
They would starve this winter.
Some said she was to blame, she brought bad luck.
They said that they should run her out of town.
But, in truth, no one dared approach her.
Grief has its own perimeter.
And so they placed seven stones around the boundary of her grief
And they called it her sanctuary:
A place set apart from the world of men
So that grief and loss and death
Might not interfere with them
And their affairs.

2. Hypsipyle

will you stop crying baby, please?

A baby starts crying.

Not again!

Baby continues to cry, mobile rings.

Will you stop crying for a minute, please!

*Baby goes silent. Mobile continues to ring,
speaker answers it.*

Yes?
I mean hello?
I mean hello, yes?

O, it's you Polls, hi.

No, my one's finally gone down.
I swear, he's like one of those dolls that cry
When you pull the cord,
Only my one's cord seems to go on for ever.

Beat.

Christ I'm bored.

I mean, we came here to broaden our horizons didn't we?

Have some fun?

Not wipe the arse of Her Royal Highness of Harvard's son.

I mean we gave them their civilisation, didn't we?

Long before they were God's own nation they were ours,

I remember that much from history.

Then there was some argument about tea,

And now I've got to get her brat's tea every night.

It's not right,

I'm telling you it's not.

What about your lot, they gone down?

I don't know how you do it.

Three!

My one's enough for me.

So what are your plans then, while they are asleep?

Relax and read her Cosmo in the bath?

Clean the kitchen?

Christ yours are having a laugh.

Her Royal Highness wouldn't dare, I swear.

Twelve hours each day I spend with her son,

Then she says she doesn't want me taking showers in working hours,

Or talking on the phone all the time,

Even though I'm all alone –

Yes, apart of course from you, Polls.

But we're in the same boat, aren't we?

Christ, we're only just eighteen,

Barely old enough to vote

And far from home.

She always treats me like a child, you know,

Telling me what time she wants me in at night,

Says she wants me rested,

So that I might 'discharge my duties to the best

Of my abilities'.

Sorry to go on Polls, but sometimes she really gets on my tits.

She's never done complaining

About everything little thing;

The way I dress him,

Says I dress him up too much,

And am always changing him,

That he's not a doll.

'You wouldn't treat your own like that,' she says.

'No,' I say, 'but I wouldn't get a bloody foreigner to look after my own
    neither.'

That shuts her up, for a moment,

But then she gets all huffy.

Christ I can't win.

'Just keep it simple from here on in,

One babygro per day, okay?'

If she wants everything to be just so,

Let her give up her job and stay at home,

That's what I say,

Then she'll know how hard it is.

I swear, Polls, my one barely knows which one of us his mother is.

Baby is crying. She tries to ignore it this time.

Yeah, he's off…

No, no Polls, don't go.
Let him cry it off, he'll soon get tired of it…

Yeah…

No…

Sure…

Yeah…

And speaking of back home –

Well I was, before…

Yeah, well you'll never guess who I met in town last night –

Yeah, yeah him you're right.
How'd you guess?
Fancy seeing him over here,

That's what I call coincidence.

No, I suppose that makes sense.

Well, he looks so much better than he did at school,
Shorter hair, less spots, and he's got tall…

Yeah, and, you know, lean.

Yeah…

Yeah…

No, all I mean is –

Where? Last night?
I met him in the old town, near the square.
You know, in front of the big church –

Cathedral, whatever, anyway, there.
And with the World Series, the place was going mad,
Apparently this is the best chance the Sox have ever had.
Or something.
And everyone was out in fancy dress –

Well, Halloween, I guess.
The place was in a party mood
It was great,

What I got to see of it.
HRH did not get back till after eight –

Baby is crying.

Not again.
Will you just stop your crying baby please –

No, Polls, don't go.
Yeah, he's fine, I'm sure.
Where was I?
Yeah, because of HRH I got there late –

Well, not a date exactly, no.
I mean nothing's happened yet,
But you never know.
What's the saying? Out of little acorns –

No, I don't have to go,
He's fine.
You know my one he cries all the time.
What, Polls, what?
I missed that –
Jesus would you ever stop!

No, we didn't go far.
Just some quiet bar.

Yeah he has, finally, Jesus –

No, I don't know the name.
What does the name matter?
You know the kind of place:
Pitchers of beer, burgers, baseball on the box,
Good old boys in caps all cheering for the Sox.
It was a laugh, like I said.

What?

No.

*The Speaker gradually shifts her focus from the mobile to a
cross examiner.*

Nothing happened.
I told you.

He was crying all morning.
Off his food.

What does she know?
She sees him for five minutes then she's off to work.
Eventually I got him down.
But ten minutes later he was off again.

No,
I did what I always did,
I lifted him from his cot
And walked around with him.
I walked around with him a lot.
It seemed like he would never stop.
Shake him? No.
But then,
Then…

What?

Then he went quiet.
No. Not to sleep.
Quiet. His eyes open.
But like glass,
Like little beads,
Like the ones I used to make necklaces with as a girl.
He barely breathed –

Yes, of course I find it frustrating when a baby cries
And there's nothing you can do to comfort them,
But I did not shake him, I swear.
No, not even in frustration.
Not even when he was crying.

But afterwards, maybe,
When he went silent,
When I was afraid that he was dying,

Maybe I shook him then.

'Tell me, tell me little one what is wrong with you?

Tell me, tell me what am I to do.'

And some sick dribbled out.

And I kissed him,

And breathed into his mouth,

And pumped his little chest,

And wrapped him up to keep him safe

From all dangers.

Just as I once did with my dolls.

My little one, who was my own in every way

Except he was not mine.

The doorbell rings.

O Polls, what am I to do?

Will you stop crying baby please?

Jesus, must I listen to you for all eternity?

3. Medea

every blooming thing

Sunday morning,
The week before Christmas,
Late, eleven-thirty, twelve,
For the first time in an age
I've had a lie-in in bed.
I'd not slept in what seemed like months or years,
But that night, in my childhood room,
That night I'd slept like the dead.
But that means that now
I'm running late,
And since there'll be no time later on,
And they'll be tired and hungry
By the time he brings them back,
I'm making them their tea
Before I go on into town.
And I am hoping everything has gone okay,
But I must not think about it,
I must take things day by day.

Cheese sandwiches, with the crusts cut off,
White bread.
I've tried getting them to eat brown,
But they complain,
And say brown's not so much fun,
And they won't eat it,
And I hear myself say:
'You're only young once anyway.'

And I open some crisps
And spread them as a garnish on the plate.
But wait, they'll go stale if I leave them in the open air.
Where's this Mum keep her blooming cellophane?
I must think.
Drawer. Which drawer?
The drawer beside the sink.

Doorbell rings.

'Can you get it, Mum?'
I've got to finish up in here,
And brush my hair, and go to the loo.

I find the cellophane,
And stretch it tight across the sandwiches and crisps,
Then I go to the fridge.
I'd stuck the list to the door,
I must mentally work out my route
From store to store:
Woolworths first for the doll's house, wrapping paper,
And check out the price of the Nintendo DS while there.
Then across the square to M and S:
Snacks, chocolates, biscuits,
Dump them in the car.
Then, last of all, brave Argos for everything I can't get elsewhere.
Most people's idea of an afternoon in hell,
But not mine.
The first Christmas in ten years
When I'm free to buy presents for my own family
With my own money.

Sweet liberty, I think,
The first Christmas without him.
Don't think about it, just take it day by day,
For fear it might be all torn away.

'Who was it, Mum? Who rang the bell?'

And, as they enter
I notice the advent calender:
The doors for the last two days have not been opened.
A treat for them when they get back, I think,
If they can keep from squabbling.

'No, I don't understand.
I mean I understand the words,
But I just…I
Give me a moment, please…'

'What is your secret?'
Our friends used to say,
'It all comes so easily your way.'
And in the beginning it did all come so easily,
Like a game you play when you're a child.
He was a doctor, and I, a nurse,
And of course he proposed to me upon a bended knee.
Nor was he like the other men I'd known,
He seemed alive to my every need;
When I was pregnant he cooked and cleaned.

He took care of everything:
The house, the garden, the banks, the bills, the car,
Every blooming thing.
There was nothing he would not do for me,
Until there was nothing for me to do at all,
Until I realised that I could not breathe.

'You're suffocating me.'

'What do you mean?' he'd say.

'I mean I want to go back to the way we were before,' I'd say.

'Before what?' he'd say.

'Before, in the early days.
When we first started to go out.'

'How can we go back to how we were,
When we now have them to think about?'

'But why do you have to do everything for me?'

'Because I love you.'

'Your love is like a prison.'

'What do you mean?'

'I mean you always must know where I've been.'

'And do you not want to know how I spend my days?'

'And how much I pay for this or that – '

'I spend my days working, providing for my family – '

'A cab, a bus, my lunch – '

'So we can meet the repayments on the mortgage or – '

'My hair, my make-up, a magazine – '

'So I can budget for the holidays.'

'Or if I go out for a drink – '

'A drink, with whom? I said with whom?'

'It doesn't matter.'

'But you don't go out and drink alone?'

'With friends from work,' I'd say.

'Which friends,' he'd say, 'which friends?'

'Why must I tell you every thing?' I'd say,
'Every blooming thing.'

'Because you are my wife,' he'd say.

'For goodness' sake,' I'd say, 'get a life
And give me back my own.'

And then one night you awake,
And you really cannot breathe.

He is kneeling on your chest,

His ankle bones digging into your tummy and –

Smack!

Across your face and –

Smack again!

And in the background your child cries:

'Please, Daddy, please stop hitting Mummy.'

And he hears him, and he sighs,

Like a judge who, with great regret,

Must hand down his severest sentence yet.

He shakes his head and picks up the boy,

And with him in his arms, turns to you and says:

'Say goodnight now son, you need your rest.'

You get his meaning, he means: 'watch what you do

Or next time it will be him instead of you.'

So as he takes him back to bed,

You lie quite still,

While a thousand useless thoughts

Career around your head.

And he returns and this time takes care to lock the door

Before he drags you to the floor,

And straddles your chest,

And pins you down and with hot breath hisses in your ear:

'Whore!'

And smacks you again, but you don't struggle anymore.

You let him,

So he won't hurt them.

And afterwards you lie quite still,

Staring at the ceiling,

Feeling nothing.

From now on you will do what he says,
For their sake, you will take the beatings.

'No, my mother did not put me up to it
She simply made me see.'

'Whore!'
'No, there's no one else.
If you must blame someone, blame yourself.'
'Whore! Worse than whore! I will kill you, I will.'
And I said: 'Fine, kill me if you want, I don't care,
I don't care anymore.'
'But if he kills you,' my mother'd said, 'what will become of them?'
That's how she had convinced me in the end,
That's when I knew something must be done.
That was a Sunday morning too,
I remember, the sky was blue, clear blue.
I took them and the cordless phone
Into the garden, down the end to where,
Huddled tightly together behind an old apple tree,
We could hide.
I shook as I dialled.
It rang and rang,
For what seemed like forever.
'Mummy! Mummy! Please come and rescue me!'

'Coward! Bitch! Cunt! Whore!'

'I don't care what you call me anymore.'

'I made you what you are.'

'I'm not afraid of you.'

'You would be nothing now if not for me.
I'm warning you.
Who puts the food upon the table?
The roof over your head?
Who pays for the sheets and pillows
Upon our marriage bed?
The same bed on which you lie
Legs spread for your lover boy.'

'There is no one else, there is just us.'

'And now you go and make all this fuss?'

'Please, you're not well, please get away from us.
My mother and the police will be here soon.'

'Your mother is a whore too…'

And that and probably more, much more, he said.

They found me face down in a flower bed,
Bits of earth and stone and glass in the back of my head.
I felt nothing any more.
With handcuffed hands he hammered
On the car roof, before we sped away.
'I hate you, I hate you and your happy future,' I heard him say.
'You'll not wipe me from your history so easily,
You'll not deny me access to my family,
You'll pay for this, you'll pay!'

Doorbell.

Sunday,
The week before Christmas,
Eleven, eleven-thirty, twelve,
And I have their tea prepared
Before I go on into town,
When the police call round.
'What is it?' I hear myself say,
Though I'm doing my best not to think,
Concentrating on the day to day,
The advent calendar, or radio, or the tap dripping in the sink –
'You had best sit down.'
'What is it?' I say again,
Though I know I do not want to know.
'There's no easy way to say this.'
'What is it? Is it him?'
The earth beneath my feet is draining away,
I feel as though I am sinking down.
They place a broken box in front of me.
The old cedar chest they used
To hoard their priceless treasure:
Beads, buttons, and tinsel crowns,
Old cracker jokes and frayed silk scarves,
But all that they contain now are their two christening gowns.
'No, I don't understand.
I mean I understand the words.
But I just…I…'
My children, my children, tell me where they are?
'Your husband – '
'Your former husband – '

' – with a pyjama cord – '

Down through the floor.

Down into the ground.

My clothes are suffocating me.

Fire burns from my head.

My dress, my clothes, eat my flesh,

My skin melts like teardrops from my bones –

'Then jumped from a window on the seventh floor…'

I cannot breathe, yet I am not dead.

' – with this box in his arms.'

How am I to live after this day?

And the last thing that I see before I am gone completely

Is their tea.

And all I can think of is the waste

Of the sandwiches and the crisps,

And Christmas lists,

And of every blooming thing.

4. Alcestis

the finest thing

Anybody who was anybody
Came to the Thessaly back then.
The Friday nights were legendary;
You'd see Noel and Liam and Posh and Becks,
Richard and Judy and Ant and Dec,
Peter O'Toole and Richard Harris,
Michael Portillo and Matthew Parris,
Tracey Emin and Damien Hirst,
Georgie Best and his unquenchable thirst,
Archer and Aitken before they were sent down,
Barrymore and friend, before the friend drowned,
Pete and Kate in the corner drinking champagne,
Then off to the toilet once more…what a pain.
And Boris Becker and his peccadilloes,
And Jordan and those…well those pillows,
And Robbie and one of his young female fans,
And Blunkett and Prescott and their wandering hands,
And Pierce, Pierce Brosnan, my favourite Bond,
And the latest one, Daniel Craig, the Bond who went blond,
And Scarlett and Jennifer and Sarah Jessica with all their teeth and
their hair,
And Max Clifford, Max Clifford of course, was everywhere.
All of them came when they were in town,
My husband's hospitality was world renowned.
And when at last the kitchen was closed
He'd come and sit and talk with them.
'Talk to them as though they're gods,' he'd say,

'As if nothing of the claims
Of human or of natural law pertained to them.
Talk to them as if they and their fame were immortal.'
That's how he'd talk to them and drink champagne,
Table after table, night after night,
He imbibed celebrity,
As if there were no tomorrow,
As if he too was a god…

But then tomorrow came.
His mortal frame could take no more;
His liver began to fail.

And, given his lifestyle, his age,
The late nights, the alcohol, the rich food,
The chances of a transplant were not particularly good.
He joked with these celebrities
That the source of his success was the cause of his disease,
But mostly he hid his pain as best as he was able,
And kept it light and witty;
Mortality has no place at fame's table.

Yet one of them must have had some pity
And told him of a new procedure:
Partial liver transplant from a living donor;
Although it's not common practice yet –
In fact, doctors advise against it.
They say it's wrong to operate upon the healthy –
But it's on the rise,
Which is hardly a surprise,

When waiting lists are long
And people are wealthy;
People will do anything for one more day of life.

But the question was who?
After all, who is willing to give part of themselves for you?
And this was major surgery,
Though the chances of fatality,
For the living donor, were one in two hundred.

He first went to his parents;
'Father, Mother, I am your only son,
And no parent wants to outlive their child,
And both of you are old,
Would you not take this risk for me?'
'Son,' his father replied,
'You know that we are proud of you,
Your wealth, your fame,
You have entertained princes, presidents and premieres,
Your restaurant is renowned around the world,
You are the light of our dimming eyes,
But we cannot do what you ask us to.'

He asked his partner in the Thessaly;
'I'm dying, my friend, this is the only hope,
And if I die, the Thessaly dies too.
Do this and I'll make over half my share to you.'
'I'm afraid, I must pass on this proposal,' his partner said,

'What profiteth the man of business profit, if he be dead?'
He even asked a few of the celebrities
Who'd bid him join them at an evening's end,
And ply him with compliments,
And try to ply his glass.
But they would mutter their sympathies,
Finish their drinks and leave.
And he would curse himself and call himself a fool
For having broken his own house rules.

And yet still he would not come to me,
Nor would he have except our son,
Our only child, then in his teens,
Who looked up to him as a god,
Persuaded him.
At least that's how it appeared to me
When they came to me together,
As I was doing the weekly inventory
One Monday afternoon in the cellar;
Son in front, father shuffling behind,
Hand upon his shoulder, seeming so much older
As he caught his breath in the watery light.

'We're short on ninety-seven Pomerol,
And ninety-nine Lafitte,' I called to him.

'Mum,' replied my son,
'Dad's something to ask you.'

'What is it?'

My husband hesitated.
Perhaps he could see what my son could not,
That if I, his wife, refused,
The request would lie between us like a knife.

'I know that I've no right
To ask this of you,
And if you refuse, I'll understand.
And I know that I've brought this upon myself;
My love of the finer things, of company,
And you are finer than the finest thing, to me,
The best of company,
And life without you would not be worth the living…'

'Then why ask me?'

'Because you are the only hope I have.'

He began to cry.

'Because I do not want to die.'

'And the chances of something going wrong, Mum,
They're so small,' said my son.
'Scientific advances mean no one has to die at all.'

He passed me articles from the internet.

'No one else will help me,' my husband said,
'Not friends, not family.'

I scanned the documents;
Procedure, time between assessment and recovery…

'But what if something should go wrong?
Who will then care for our son?'

'Nothing will go wrong, Mum, science – '

'I want to see our son grow up too,' my husband said,
'I want to see our son grow up along with you.'

        Beat.

'Ok,' I said.

        Beat.

'So you'll do this for me, you'll save my life?'

'I am your wife.'

My husband and my son embraced me.

'How could I have asked you this?'

'Because you are afraid.'

'But you're doing it because you want to? Say it is.'

'She's doing it because she loves you, Dad.'

'I'm doing it so you might see.'

'See what?' he asked.

'You'll see when you can see.
And you must promise me that if I die – '

'You won't,' they both said.

'That you'll not take another wife,
Fall for one of your celebrities.'

'How could I?'

'A new wife always hates the children of the old.'

'None of them could take your place
In my home or heart.'

'You have not met every woman yet.'

'I promise then, I promise.
If you die, which you won't,
Not only shall no woman take your place,
No more late nights with celebrities for me,
The days of *legendary hospitality* are over,
I shall work hard and mourn you always.
But there is no danger of this happening,
You'll be fine.
And I know about the finer things.'

'My son, you are the witness,
Your father shall take no wives or mistresses,
And shall honour my memory always.'

I took my husband's hand,
And placed it upon the head of his child.

'Love him always,' I said.

'And I'll love the giver as I love the gift,' he replied.

We made the appointment at the hospital,
We did the tests and we were,
As I always knew we'd be, compatible.
The date was set and,
Being private, soon arrived.
We dropped our son at my parents,
And drove to the hospital in silence,
Where they prepared us for the operation.

I did not manage to count past five.
Next thing I knew I had floated free
Above the surgeons and the table,
I watched the operation that they performed on me.
I knew that I was still alive
Because I was tied by a silver thread,
But after they'd removed half of my liver
They got into difficulties.
I'd bled internally.
They worked in a quiet frenzy
To find and staunch the flow
And then a nurse shouted that I was coming-to,

And the anaesthetist adjusted my dose,
And again time fell away from me,
And next thing that I saw
Was myself being wheeled down the corridor
To intensive care,
To where my still unconscious husband lay.
And there, still tied by the silver thread
To my sleeping self,
I watched over us both as we slept.

And I watched on as he came round,
And waited all that day,
In a post-operative haze
Of joy and gratitude for his delivery,
For me to do the same.
Then all the next day
I watched him from somewhere up around the ceiling,
As his feelings of apprehension and guilt grew,
And on the third day I watched as he lay
With the bitter taste of dread in his mouth,
Not knowing what to say or do.

'How can I live without you?'

I watched him as he watched me,
Until the doctors no longer deemed it
Conducive to his recovery.
He was moved to a general ward,
And I stayed there in my hospital bed

Looking at myself as my life,
I suppose, dangled by this thread.
Though I felt no fear,
And I could hear and understand
All that was said to me,
My only frustration being that I could not reply.

'How can I live without you?'

My husband would say
Every day he visited me.

'I should have been the one to die.'

But I could tell that he was slowly getting well,
And I wanted to tell him that I was happy for that,
And proud.
And when my son came and cried,
And said that it was all his fault,
I wanted to reassure him that it had been my choice,
That I was happy for him too,
That he still had his father,
And that I hadn't gone away,
And that I loved when he came to me each day,
And told me all his news.
But he'd say, 'what is the use?'
That I could not hear,
That it was scientifically unlikely
That I was even there

Under any of the criteria by which identity's defined,
And now he never could say sorry,
And all these visits did was remind him of what I'd been,
And what he'd lost.
And I would reach out to try and touch him,
But the arms of the immortal soul
Are things of insubstantiality.
If only you could hear me, he'd say.
If only you could hear me too, I'd say in return.
And he would leave,
Alone with his grief.

And after some time
I was moved to a hospital
That specialised in cases such as mine.
My husband left hospital too,
The surgeon deciding that he
Would soon be well enough to resume work at the Thessaly.
Consequently he came to see me less often.
My son came less often too.
In truth their visits lit my days,
Without them, my soul would drift for whole afternoons,
Evenings, nights,
Time lost its shape entirely.
Perhaps this is what it's like to die,
To simply drift off, up and away,
Out of memory,
But I could never let go completely
Of the silver thread connecting me
To that body in that bed.

Then something aroused my soul
From its sleep upon the ceiling,
The squeal of the duty nurse, to be precise,

'James Bond!'

James Bond it seemed was in the building.
Not the new one, the blond,
No, the Irish one, Pierce Brosnan.
And he had asked her where I was,
And with him were my husband and my son,
And Pierce came in and sat down
And told them to sit down too,
And sheepishly they did as he bid them do.
And he explained that he had been in town,
And stopped by the Thessaly to eat
To see how my husband was,
And he had found him greatly changed;
Tanned, looking younger and thinner,
He looked like a million dollars, and after dinner,
Pierce asked him to join him like the good old days,
But my husband told him those days, and their goodness, were gone.

'What's wrong?' said Pierce, 'you can tell me,
I am James Bond, or at least I used to be.
Your son, is he okay?'

'Yes, my son is fine.'

'Your mother and your father?'

'Still alive though we don't talk much anymore.'

'Your wife? I missed her pretty face,
Is she not on tonight?
Is everything all right with you and her?'

'My wife…
Is fine. We're still together.
Just someone who I used to know, I lost.'

'Someone close?' asked Pierce.

Beat.

'No.'

'In that case you'll join me for a glass.'

In short, Pierce told me as I slept,
That my husband sat and had a drink with him,
More out of duty than conviviality.
And every day that week, Pierce ate at the Thessaly,
And, each evening when the kitchen closed,
My husband would sit and drink with him.

The first night he had just the one,
The second two, the next three,
And so on.
Not that he cheered up much, said Pierce, nor the staff.

'Chirst, what's wrong with this place?
It used to be a laugh.
What is wrong with everyone?
Are you going to spend your lives mourning the loss
Of some old girlfriend of the boss?
I myself lost my first wife
And she did not want me to spend my life
Mourning her.'

That's when my husband had had to say, 'Pierce
About that old girlfriend, a word…'

And he told Pierce what had occurred.

'My friend, my friend,' said Pierce, 'why did you lie to me?
Did you fear you might offend?
You are justly famed for your hospitality,
But this is hospitality to a fault.
What's more you swore to keep sacred her memory,
And each night you drank more
Upon this your new liver?
While the giver, your wife
Lies in a coma in her hospital bed,
Her life hanging by a thread.
We must go visit her.'

'No, I can't bear to,' my husband said,
'I've tried to reach her, but she is gone,
The doctors say she's there, but she does not respond.
It would be easier if she were dead.'

'She's there,' said Pierce,
'I have experience in these things,
Have you not heard of the silver thread?'

And so Pierce Brosnan, my husband and my son
Came to visit me that night in my hospital bed,
And searched the room for the silver thread
That tied my body to my soul.

'It's here somewhere,' Pierce said,
'Though very hard to see.'

And as they hunted he told them to talk to me.
And they did.
At first with difficulty,
And then the words began to flow
As spring's first sun melts the winter's snow
And it trickles down the mountain first in rivulets,
Then in streams that teem into a brook,
Then torrents that feed broad rivers.
And when they'd said all that they'd not dare say before,
Their worst fears, they too felt a kind of spring arrive,
And they dried their tears
And turned to trivialities;

Who had been in this day or that,
Who'd lost weight and who was fat,
Who was in and who was out,
And what was that dress all about?
The way that we had talked and laughed about the week
Over the Sunday lunch.
And my soul delighted in their stories
Of celebrities,
Whose sole purpose, is to entertain us mortals –
And then my husband cried 'I see, I see!'

'What do you do see?' Pierce said.

'The silver thread.'

'Gently, gently pull it in as you might a fragile kite.'

My husband did. And gently Pierce asked him:
'Is that all you now see?'

'No,' my husband said,
'I see that no one else can die for me.'

And next thing that I knew I was blinking
From my own eyes, in my own body,
And blindly looking at the ceiling,
And Pierce Brosnan was somewhere in the background saying:
'You see now what every man must see, my friend;

Necessity.

There is no such thing as immortality,

Except, perhaps, upon a silver screen.'

5. Phedra

what have I said?

What time is it?

That late?
And the moors are dark and I am in a state.
Again.
Hold me.
I mean, hold up my head,
My strength has melted quite away.
Let my hair fall free about my shoulders.
I'm burning up, I'm burning up in here.
To be out there, out on the moors,
To kneel by a waterfall or stream,
To drink in the clear, fresh water,
To lie once more under the poplar trees,
Not locked up in this dark room,
The prison of my passion, my tomb.
Let me go outside up to the fells,
To the forests of tall pine,
To where the hunters chase the wild deer.
I'd like to ride with them, why shouldn't I?
Crashing through the trees,
My horse snapping and cracking everything in its path,
As the hounds bay at its heels,
My hair glinting in the wind.

No, I have not had too much,
I have not had half enough.
Fill me up.

I'm sorry.
Sorry.
You must think me mad.

Then other times I see myself as the frightened deer,
Whose skin is scratched and cut
With bramble and with thorns
As it runs this way and that,
Trying to avoid the hunter's lethal shots.
So many and such strange fantasies
Chase through the forests of my mind.
Am I the hunter or the hunted?
I cannot trust myself.
I worry what I might say next.
What I have said already?
I'm afraid to think.
I dare not think.
That is why I need another drink.

Of course, I blame my mother,
Your grandmother –
Step-grandmother, I should say.
She was just the same.
What am I saying? The same!
My mind might be pit of swill and shame –

But my hands are clean,
My hands, as yet, are clean –

What do I mean?
No, you can't ask me what I mean.
You must not ask me what I mean,
I will never tell you.
To say it would be the end.
I fear what I've already said.
I must…I must…

I must hold up my head!
That is what I must do.
Now what was it I was saying to you?
My mother, your step-grandmother,
That was it, of course,
Yes.
I was saying that you might think I'm a fool for my…desires –
Don't ask.
You might think that I have no propriety,
Am obscene, even,
But she was worse than me, much worse;
My mother conceived a passion
For the hind legs of a horse.

No, this time you may ask me what I mean.
I can speak quite freely of my mother's shame,
After all, as I said, she is to blame.

No, it was not an eventer, nor a racer.
Nor a hunter, nor a steeplechaser, no,
Nor dreyhorse, nor ploughhorse, nor shirehorse
Nor any kind of workhorse
But the white horse of Pilkington.
No, not the one upon the hill,
But the one who used to lead the annual procession play
From house to house on New Year's Day;
Him.

That's it. A pantomimish kind of thing.
It had been performed for centuries,
And my uncle, a ploughman,
He was master of the ceremonies
And took the part of the horses backside.
And the procession would always start outside
The house of the mayor, and my father,
A great bull of a man, was mayor of Pilkington
For what seemed like life,
And every year the passion of his wife,
As she watched the horse perform its fertility dance
For the coming spring, grew and grew.
Her desire would not be denied
However hard she tried.

So she dreamed up the strangest plan,
She begged my uncle, the ploughman,
For a part in the procession play.

And what part would the lady mayoress care to try? He said.

I want, she replied, I want...

Need I say more?

Instead of the dance of fertility that year,
The good people of Pilkington were greeted with the sight
Of a horse's front ploughed by a horses rear.
That was the last year of the procession play,
And my parents, your stepgrandparents' marriage;
And the beginning of my shame.
And I always swore that I would not be the same.

No, I'm telling you this so you will hate me.
No, I'm telling you this so you will see
That I know what it means to bring shame upon a family,
I know how it feels.
And I'll kill myself before I do that.
I'm telling you this so you won't think
That I'm that bad. Or as mad as her.
Give me another drink.

I just need to drink when your father's not around.

Why? Don't ask.

Yes, I have a problem, yes.

With you, yes.

No, it is not going to go away.
No, I cannot say. I will not say.

No.

No, don't say that.

No, don't say that.
Of course, I like the way you eat and dress,
And play the guitar,
And ride your motorbike,
And have your music up too loud.
I like it,
I love the way you do every bloody thing.
Is it not natural that I do?
You're young,
You are your father's son.
I fell for him, is it not natural that I should fall –

Well, he's away, always away,
What am I to do?
Forced to share the same house,
The same space,
The same air as you?
Is it not natural that I have begun to care for you?
And not as a mother,
Why should I care for you as a mother,
When I'm not her?
Nor are we blood relatives,
Nor do you have a wife or significant other.
You are free,
We are free,

Except that I am married to your father,
But I want you as the hunter wants his kill.
I am ill, I know.
Hold me,
Hold me by the head
I can hold it up no longer.
Stroke my hair.

What have I said?
I am afraid to think what I have said.

Yes.

Yes.

Yes,
I am all of that and more.

I am not worthy of your father, no.
I am shameful, shameful –
I'm sorry.
Forgive me.

What have I said?

Yes, you must go to bed,
You have an early start.

I'll stay here.

Let me drink,
Let me drink and not think
Or feel anything anymore.

Let me hide myself from the sun.

6. Creusa

how can I keep quiet anymore?

It was spring,

Nineteen ninety-one,

When it became apparent that something must be done.

It was at a party, to be exact.

At an old friend's in Islington

Brant and his wife,

Who, in spite of all their wealth –

Brant was an architect

And she, whom I did not really know,

She had a boutique in Marylebone –

But, in spite of their Mercedes, the foreign holidays, the works of art
and their beautiful home,

They had been trying for a child for years in vain.

They'd tried everything, from IVF and Bach Flower Remedies,

To a traditional Chinese treatment for fertility.

They'd even been to see a holy man in Brazil

Who could reach his hand right inside of you and,

Without knife or tool, make you whole.

But to no avail.

They returned home with just themselves

And in their back yard built a shrine,

To the child that they would never have.

It even had an omphalos or navel stone

Which looked like a giant onion ring

I thought, as I stood there looking at it, sipping my white wine.

Or perhaps I was being a bit unkind.

And you had to hand it to them,
Brant and his wife, they were doers,
So they decided to adopt and,
Since the scandal of the orphanages was then in the news,
And because the rules were not so strict,
And because waiting lists did not come into it,
They decided to adopt from Romania.
So after a few fact-finding trips,
And several handfuls of dollars pressed into the appropriate fists,
They went to an orphanage and chose their son
And this party was to celebrate his arrival home to Islington.

'Look at him, look at him,' said Brant's wife,
'Isn't he the sweetest thing?'

He lay motionless in his Moses basket in the yard
Staring at the sky.
A chorus of women replied
In coos and clucks and sighs.
I'd learnt to perform most parts in life with plausibility,
But this was one I could never play convincingly.

'You should see the conditions,
That they keep them in out there,' Brant's wife went on,
'Pig sties, I swear.
It was so difficult to choose just one,
But with our lifestyles
We could not have provided a home for any more.

Yet you cannot just stand by,
So it's become our new monomania:
We've set up an organisation
To help with the adoption of children from Romania.
And we expect you all to give generously.'

'Trust you and Brant,' a chorus member said,
'To make not just a virtue, but a whole charity of your necessity.'
And everyone laughed and exchanged looks,
And reached into their handbags for their chequebooks.
But I, I just kept looking at that little boy,
So calm and self-contained and old beyond his years,
And I could not help but think of my own, so many years ago –

'He's lovely, isn't he?'
Brant's wife said to me.

'Yes, yes he is,' I replied.

'So stoical, so accepting of what life throws at him.
He never cries.'

I did not know what to do or say,
My glass was empty, I reached for a canapé.

'Just look at his little fingers, his little toes,
His brown eyes and his button of a nose.'

I looked at his fontanelle,
Beating like a second heart.
Let me cover it, I thought,
Let me protect you from all hurt.

'I'm so happy,
I'm so happy for you and Brant,'
I managed to get out.

'Go on, Clare,' she said,
'You can hold him if you want.'

I froze.
I could not speak.
And your smell, I thought, the smell of the hair upon your head,
That lasted the longest –

'No, no he's happy where he is,' I said.

I only have to close my eyes and breathe in –

'But it's good for him, the psychologist said, he needs to be held.'

I only have to close my eyes and breathe in,
And I can smell your hair again –

'He needs affection'

And you are there –

'Clare?'

'Yes, I'm sorry, yes?'

'Pick him up.'

Shakes head.

'But I trust you.'

But I don't trust me, I thought,
I've already had one taken away from me,
I dare not lose another.

'But Clare,' I heard her say, 'you'd make such a brilliant mother.
We should get you a Romanian baby of your own.'

And, standing in that garden, by that shrine in Islington,
I felt as though I'd fallen through the floor of the world once more.

'Do something,' I told myself,

'Do something so she won't suspect.'

'Do what?'

'Smile.'

'Pathetic.'

'Inspect the empty glass, the canapé.'

'What is it?

What on earth is this?

Goat's cheese dressed with pomegranate seeds?

What now?'

'Count them, count the seeds.'

'One,'

'So you can breathe;'

'Two,'

'So you can breathe;'

'Three…'

Since I had been a girl of seventeen

It had been happening to me;

The sensation of the ground giving way,

Of tumbling down into the abyss.

But recently it had been happening more often.

In Leeds a few years before on tour,

As I browsed the self-help section of a bookstore,

I saw, through the window,

A crowd of boys waiting at a bus stop outside.

Because they would have been the same age as him,

Out of habit I scanned their faces

For any hints or traces or resemblances –

'God, God, what do I do?'

Standing a bit apart from the group

Not isolated, but calm and self-contained –

There was something about his air, his gait,

I knew, I just knew,

Though the odds were infinitisimal,

This boy had to be my son.

'God, tell me, what do I do?

Do I go up to him and talk to him?

Do I follow him and stalk him?

What if he doesn't know?

What if his parents haven't told him?

Or have told him lies

That I never loved him or that I'd died?

God, please tell me what to do?

My family have not spoken of it since,

I have no one to go to for advice.'

But God did not reply.

And I thought I must be going mad,

Thinking that He might,

Seeing the son that I once had

In every schoolboy who stands at every bus stop.

The bus arrived, and they got on.

The panic and the hope subsided,

He was gone.

'…six, seven.'

There were seven pomegranate seeds,

And I was still at this party,

Trying to distract myself with miscellanea

While the women talked about adopting from Romania.

And so it did not seem strange that I did not speak,

I took a bite out of the canapé

Just as I heard one of the women's chorus say:

'Orphans
Now orphans I can understand,
But what I simply cannot comprehend
Is how any woman in her right mind
Could give away her child,
No, in most things I am a liberal, but that,
It's just unnatural.'

And by that shrine in that Islington back yard
All those years of silent hurt
And self-control and acting,
Acting as if nothing had occurred,
When I was seventeen,
That I'd never brought a baby into this world,
I spat out the canapé
With its goats cheese and pomegranate seeds,
I could no longer stay buried in the ground.
'My soul, how can I keep quiet anymore?
Why should I cover up my shame
While those whose is the greater shame
Might live without responsibility?'

'What is it?' the women's chorus said, 'what is it Clare?'

I closed my eyes and I was there.

It was late afternoon,
The sun shone on his golden hair
Making it appear that he wore a golden crown.

He came to me as I was picking yellow flowers
On the moors above our town.
He shouted at me from a distance to stay
As if he wanted to ask the way.
So many flowers I'd picked
That I'd made a basket of my dress.
Perhaps it was the sight of my bare white legs,
Or the petals stuck to my skinny chest
That made him want me.
But when he breathlessly drew near,
He grabbed me by the bloodless wrists
And dragged me as I cried for help
Into a cave where he pushed me to the ground.
As he lay himself on top of me, he rasped in my ear
'Shut up with your tears
Shut up, not a word, or I'll have to hurt you.'

'Who was he?' asked a chorus member, 'We don't follow.'

'A man! God Almighty! Phoebus Apollo!
It doesn't matter who it was.
What matters is I had a son
With little fingers, little toes
Beautiful brown eyes, a little nose,
Whom I loved.
But he was taken away from me.'

'Given up for adoption?' asked a chorus member,
'Look, I'm really, really sorry, Clare,' said the original offender.

But I never could give him up

Though I was told that if I hid my baby's birth

That one day it would be better,

That I'd have children of my own.

He was my own

And I've never had another.

And in my mind

Lord knows in my mind I went to that cave a hundred times,

And left my son on that cruel bed

On which he was conceived.

I tried to leave the memory of him there,

There for dogs to eat,

So that the pain might go away.

But it won't.

And it is me

Who has lived my life inside the cave,

Listening to the voices of the dead,

Playing out their sad stories in my head,

Living on the dry, bitter seeds,

Hating the God or gods who did this to me.

I am the slave girl who let the baby die,

I am the mother robbed of her future,

I am the wife who died so her husband might see,

I am woman who has loved injudiciously,

I am the mother who sits upon a rock alone,

I am that girl who fell down a hole

And did not come up for twenty years or more.

And then I hear one of you say

How could any woman give her child away?

'I said I'm really sorry, Clare, I swear – '

'The fact that women do give their children away
Does not mean they can,' I said to her.
'No, I am sorry,
Grief has its own boundaries
And you weren't to know you'd encroached on mine.'

And I sat down upon a rock
In that Islington back garden shrine
And I began to see
That girl whom I had always pictured in my mind
Down in the underworld,
Under the ground
Like some lost Persephone,
Was me, or the part of me I'd lost at seventeen.
And now, now she was coming back to me.
I wept.
And held her closely to my breast.

7. Demeter

the seven storeys

And so I tracked him down,
The child that I had had at seventeen,
The child that I'd not been allowed to keep.
That much of the foregoing is true,
If facts are what most interest you.
And he had agreed to meet.
I want to say that he was pleased,
I so wanted him to be pleased to meet with me,
But really, I did not know.
All they said was that he would,
And I had for so long forbidden hope
And learned to live with the bad
And comfort myself with the little good there was to be had,
That all I told myself up to that day was:
At least he is alive and well
And prepared to meet.

Now the moment had arrived,
And at the time agreed, he rang the downstairs bell
And, without asking who it was, or saying 'Hello, come in,'
Or hearing his response, or voice,
I buzzed him in.
And, as he climbed the seven flights up to my door,
Standing on the landing,
His baby bootees in my hand,
All that I had left of him,
I lived the seven longest moments of my life.

Firstly I thought, it has arrived,

The moment that you've waited for

For what seems all your life,

The moment that you never thought could happen, has come!

But then, I thought, what if I pass out in his arms,

Is that any way for him

To be reunited with his mum?

The humiliation!

O my god, I then thought, what if he really hates me

And only has agreed to see me to humiliate me?

To pay me back for having given him away?

I cannot bear the thought of losing him again.

Then I thought, anyway

How could I fit his image of what his mother ought to be?

Twenty-one years of dreams and fantasies,

I'm bound to disappoint.

O God, I then thought, what if he's a disappointment?

What if he's dull or ugly or violent?

I could hear him in the stairwell

Reaching the sixth landing; only one more storey –

Good god, it had never occurred to me to think, what if he's a Tory?

It's all too much, I can't go through with it, where can I hide?

I'm so afraid, I thought, I want to die.

I ran back inside my apartment and closed the door.

I cannot do this.

I must get away from here, I must go.

But where? The only option is the window

And I am on the seventh floor.

All the same, I rush to it and open it,

As he reaches my door.

I should never have started this, never,

I was much happier before –

Doorbell rings.

But as I'm thinking this there comes

Through the open window, a billow

Of warm air, a chorus of birdsong,

And, it is so long since I've known such weather,

It takes some time to see

That the afternoon burns red and gold for me,

And not even the coldest of cold winters can last forever,

And every seed must forsake the security of the earth

And take its chances in the fickle air.

And so I took a deep breath and wiped my eyes and smoothed my hair,

And prepared my smile and decided

I will smile at and I will love whatever I might meet.

I went to the door and opened it.

And standing on the welcome mat,

Greeting me with a nervous: 'Hi – '

Is a beautiful young man,

The very image of me when I was a girl,

My son returned from the underworld.

And in all my fearful thoughts

I never stopped to think that he must feel

Just as nervous and afraid as me.

But, in that recognition of each other's fear

All distance and all the years of absence disappear.

And we are whole again, we have found what is ours,

And summer returns with a golden flower.

The End.

Acknowledgements

I am grateful to the Onassis Programme at Oxford for commissioning the piece and Helen Eastman and Oliver Taplin who encouraged, coaxed and acted as midwives to so many of these tales. I am deeply indebted to Clare Higgins who gave not only so much to that initial performance, but so much of herself to the stories.

For the piece's latter incarnation as my inaugural I am grateful to Professor Hilary Fraser and the School of Arts for supporting such an ambitious 'lecture'. To Anna and Nicola in External Relations at Birkbeck, University of London, who gamely ran with the idea and organized the event on behalf of the College. To my colleagues Andrew McKinnon, and Professor Rob Swain and his Theatre Directing MFA students who lent their time, energy and expertise to this production. And to Sophie Larsmon for drawing all the many threads together.

Finally, for their love, support and belief, as ever, Madeline, Oisín and Lily.

Colin Teevan

Lightning Source UK Ltd.
Milton Keynes UK
UKHW020405261121
394626UK00007B/291

9 781783 191314